Read the two captions.
Can you match each caption
to its picture?

cod in a pan

carrots in a pot

Read the sentences. Which one
matches the picture?

Hit the bell.

Fill the pot.

9

Read the captions. Can you find the rat and the hat in the picture?

a rat as big as a cat

a red hat in a red bag

Read these captions. Can you match the captions to the pictures?

red on the rug

mess on the mat

13

Read the sentences. Can you find
the rabbit and the pup in the
picture?

The rabbit is in the hut.

The pup is in the mud.

Read the sentences. Which one matches the picture?

Get off the bus.

Get a hug and a kiss.

Read the sentences. Which one matches the picture?

A nut on the bag.

Get on top of the rock.

Read the sentences. Can you find the rabbit and the duck in the picture?

The rabbit is at the vet.

The duck is on top.

Muddy maze

Help the muddy pup get to the bath.